AF423174

I dedicate this book to the HOLY SPIRIT, my mentor and partner, and I thank the Lord Jesus Christ for giving me the privilege to share what is in this book for His kingdom and to the body of Christ.

To my loving wife Lilian and my beautiful daughters, Glory, Grace and Gift for their support and encouragement, I love you and thank you, to my brother Ernest Chukwemeka, for his contribution to this mission of spreading the love of God to humanity.

And to New Creation Outreach Church, thank you for your support and prayers.

Table of Contents

INTRODUCTION

Can you have a future without worries? Presently, most of us have moved on from the past that has met us in the present and will still follow us into the future. This carry on can be sickness, financial crisis, disappointments, failures, and other contrary situations. In this book, you will learn how to have a self-sufficient life.

It does not matter the trials, tests, persecutions, or fierceness of the storms you face. The future is beautiful to you. You are more than a conqueror. Nothing has the power to overwhelm you. The time to have a fresh atmosphere away from the impending doom tickling around the world has come in the form of this book.

There is a life outside what you are going through today. A life of upward and forward movement that is alien to sufferings and hardships awaits you. What does it take you to believe this? Faith is what you need to change your situation. Faith is the currency that defiles every law of nature. With faith, you can have a life with no business with the negative influences of this world. The time to let go of the fearful news and prediction of calamities have come. Happiness and peace of mind is a choice you make with a little guidance from this book.

By the time you finish reading 'A Future without Worries,' you will recreate the dream world you have ever desired. The time to shine and light up your world has come. Gather all those dreams that have become dormant, and take action. Your world awaits you to manifest the glory of God by freeing it from the corrupting challenges that have refused to let you live a higher life. If you had a terrible past or experience, you should not give it the power to ruin your present and future. When you show up with a new mindset of 'I am more than a conqueror, I live above the influences of this world,' the darkness and cruelty are dispelled.

You have a mandate to give beauty, meaning, and direction to your world. If it seems like you are in a dark tunnel, become the light by living in the promises of God. How do you live in a promise that you are not experiencing?

Keep affirming your right as the first-born to every good and perfect thing. You do not chicken out when there is pressure. You are the pilot of your life, and the direction you are taking from now is the success route.

"For whatsoever is born of God overcometh the world: and this is the victory that overcometh the world, even our faith." Learn to rule over circumstances with the Word of faith in your mouth. That is the essence of your existence on earth.

CHAPTER 1

When Hope Loses Its Strength

Amelia turned and stared painfully at her past, which was filled with love and laughter. If only she could turn back the hands of the clock. She once had unrestricted movement and could travel to any part of the world in hours. There was no fear of an uncontrollable virus raving the world. There was no world order to restrict her from living life to the fullest. The past was the future she had built over the years. In her world, there was no worry until now. Most of her worries could be handled with money. She was living the life she dreamed about until life fell apart for her. Life in the past was the life she wanted. Yet, she might dwell in this past for as long as she wants but cannot live in it. Today, the future looks so bleak for her. The beautiful dreams she had have gradually fizzled away. She has stopped dreaming because she has no assurance that everything will go back to what it used to be.

Most of us have similar experiences like Amelia, whose better days seemed to be in the past. But we are not going to give up. How could we crave for what we cannot taste? The outside of our world might look like things are falling apart on us, but we should not let it leave us depressed and frustrated.

It is not easy to abide in hope when difficult times arise. But God is with us even when we don't feel or see Him. He will never disappoint us because He makes all things work together for our good.

You did not come to earth as an extra or a replacement of another human. Life is not a football game, where you sit on the reserve while others play for your victory. In football, the glory and victory belong to the team, even though an individual or more might have scored the winning goals.

In life, you play to win, no matter the opponent you face. You must train like a footballer to be fit for your next game. It does not matter if you lost the last challenge; you must play to win to avoid being relegated to the loser's zone.

Interestingly, footballers play to complement each other for victory to happen. For you, you play in every wing and must coordinate yourself against the rest of the world. You must play your life game to win. You were birthed for a purpose, and your responsibility is to live out that purpose. While millions of people leave the earth without fulfillment, you cannot live an average life. It is time to unlearn and learn why you are here on earth.

God brought you on earth for a divine mandate, a life of endless miracle that swings only upward and forward only. If you are experiencing stagnation or downturns in life, it is time to make a swift 'U' turn.

These hard times are small potatoes compared to the coming good times, the lavish celebration awaiting us. You heard that right! The future has better days ahead, no matter what you feel or experience around you. There's far more in the future than meets our eye. The things we see today will be gone, and a new chapter will surely open. If the future offers us elegantly appointed life, why do we act as if we are running a rat race?

What do you believe? Have you ever planned a life better than what you once planned for your life? Do you strongly believe that your 'good' is good enough for someone like you? When you have broken pieces, crushed dreams, unfulfilled reality, a depressed spirit, worrisome personality, or collapsed lifestyle, what do you do?

Did you abandon life because you did not get it right? You are bigger than you believe in yourself. There is power in belief when it influences our actions. If you do not believe, other factors will impose their beliefs on you directly and indirectly. The power of the mind is the most potent remedy to our life challenges. We can create something out of nothing. The Wright brothers believed they could build a vehicle that would fly, and they did by trying.

What you see and hear from your beliefs. That means the information you receive has a way of transforming your life. Be careful. Negative belief creates problems for you in the near future.

God has the power to perform miracles in your life. He may not answer your prayers the way you want Him to, but He always responds. He will help you overcome the challenges you have to face.

Watch your internal conversation. You should be the moderator of the silent thoughts in your head. The voice you hear loudest is the one in your mind. No word is idle, especially the ones you use on yourself. Don't use negative labels on yourself. What you say to yourself is a way of acting through you. Even the innocent jokes you use on yourself can be an obstacle in your reality.

The world is harsh enough already. If you make a mistake, admit it and get over it fast. Then call yourself what you want to see. You are your prophet. Just like an aircraft that taxies for a short distance before it rises steeply, while it runs contrary to the wind, you must not embrace popular narratives and labels. When you do, your flight begins to struggle with the wind and gravity.

Gravity does not forgive when it forcefully drags you

down when you are 38,000 feet, about 5.9 to 7.2 miles — high in your cruising altitudes. The cruising altitude we attain in life does not have business with the fields created by others. We reach our peak when we are determined and unwavering to the corrupting narratives from others.

Reinvent yourself if you have no mind of your own. Go higher above friends' pressure. Act from your new identity to become the person you must become in life. Courage does not mean we are never scared. In the face of fear, we should show how courageous we are to remove doubt from our minds. What is courage? Courage is an ACTION in the face of fear.

The fear of failure can leave you to live an unfulfilled life. What happens if you do not take that step? Most of us have lost opportunities because we were too scared to give it a trial, especially in the work environment. Sometimes, other people's credentials can push us to the wall, compete against them, or take responsibility.

Since Rome was not built in a day, you can take up difficult challenges. The worst that might happen is that you will fall? You are thinking of the embarrassment, the narratives of others, and the time wasted, including money flushed down the drain. What if you won? What narratives will you create for yourself? What you believe controls you.

You must never accept to be ordinary. You are superhuman, discovering the powers bestowed on you. Just like the fictional Superman, who learned how to use his powers to help humankind, so are you on your journey to discovering your potential and ability to do extraordinary things.

We recognize opportunities easily when they are far off, especially in other people's lives. We talk endlessly about these opportunities and pray they come to us. We see better ways of handling such opportunities. However, they tend to shrink in size as they approach us such that we do not recognize them in our lives. Most people miss life-time opportunities because we talked to see them in small pockets. Big doors swing on small hinges. What is the small thing you can do or use today? Do or use it.

Gold is expensive! But do you know that you do not give gold its value? When we take out its impurities, gold becomes expensive. The same situation is what happens to you. For you to be valuable, you must brush away ignorance, negative labels, mediocrity, and incompetence daily. Let your true value emerge so you can affect your world for good. You have God-given value. You are special.

Success is not where you are. Success is who you are.

CHAPTER 2

Step Out of Your Shells

What happens when you board a bus, and there are no more seats for passengers? Passengers step down for another bus. However, in life, buses are different. They come in the form of vision. When you see a moving bus with the right vision, hold onto it, stand if the bus is filled, and embrace it if you cannot stand.

You must align with people with the right attitude. If your association is flawed, your movement becomes clogged with unnecessary dirt. Your life should be a testament to positivity. When you find things contrary to what you want, do not start complaining. The world is cluttered with excuses, and we should learn to get rid of them.

**Learn to walk in God's plan and stay
in the center of His will.**

Take a Walk

Sometimes things do not go as planned. Fear and anxiety can creep in take over our thoughts and influence our actions. But God offers us peace amid life's storms. Practice positive talking sessions to things around you. Speak to your finances, car, mortgage, family, health, and everything. When things around you hear positive things about them, they respond to your words.

It might take some of us time to speak differently from what we say to conditions and ourselves. It takes practice to win your world with words.

Say this:

I enter every situation with boldness and confidence, knowing that the Lord has prepared my path. I walk on preordained pathways, doing those good works, which God has predestined, for me, and I am living the good life, which He prearranged and made ready for me.

I have clarity of vision and strong focus; no darkness, no distractions, no confusion, no failure. My journey is in one direction only - upward and forward. No down days, no discouragement, no weakness; I walk the path of victory, in perpetual triumph over every adversity and every situation that confronts me.

My life will be a wonder; my testimonies will be outstand-

ing, and even I will be amazed at the outworking of God's grace in me, for the things that are impossible with men are possible with me because God is at work in me.

If you do not feel comfortable saying these words because they seem unreal, make them real to your existence. Believe that life is beautiful and you are not a stranger to good things. Your testimonies should inspire praise, your success results should evoke worship, and you will do the impossible in this life.

There is a lot of power in positive thinking but when you come to a point where you can't go any further, admitting your weaknesses to God is about the most positive thing you could do at that moment.

Take a walk away from things that do not conform to your life. You have to love yourself more to appreciate your strength. The circumstances surrounding your birth do not matter. That you were adopted or trained in a foster home has no grip on your future. You are the determinant of what the future should be for you.

When you become fearful and have negative thoughts, stop them in their tracks and turn them into something positive. Your life is too beautiful to be ruined by what others think of you, what you have done in the past, and what has happened to you.

Give yourself love and keep your eyes away from those who reject you; if you hear a no today, you will hear a yes tomorrow. When you keep your eyes on what is missing, you'll be anxious, but when you keep your eyes on what's settled, you'll be grateful.

The Success of Your Future Is Solely Dependent Upon The Departure From Your Past.

What do you do when you feel hopeless when you cast your trust on hope? Sometimes, we assume that we do not need other people to speak positively to us. We get so frustrated that we see no silver lining in our predicament.

When you find yourself in a lifeless situation that makes you feel abandoned, become the light in your tunnel. Rekindle your life by taking off the cloth of emptiness.

**Become the architect that will redesign
your situation.**

There is no hopeless situation. Every situation depends on what you see. What do you see in your present situation? What you are passing through is not new in the world. However, how you pull out of it is what makes the difference.

The Demon We Cannot Let Go

Sometimes, the past and wounds of our yesterdays can be our today's demons. While it is easy to say we have forgiven, many of us find it difficult to let go. We keep the wounds open for fresh pains. Why do we torment ourselves with something that should remain in the past?

Our wounds prevent us from avoiding the darkness of our pain. However, ineffectively and determinedly, we cannot numb it out; we try. Learn to heal from your wounds. When you have healed from your past, today and tomorrow's burdens become easier to offload.

Many of us carry excess baggage that belongs to the past. Imagine entering an airplane in the First-Class Cabin and find someone with a piece of heavy baggage on his head. The image does not sink well in your memory because it is a strange sight.

You have many questions to ask and the airline to blame for this misnomer. However, when we confront this fellow about the situation, he tells us that he cannot let go of his property from his sight. When you offer to help him drop the baggage on the floor, he screams and tells you that he is comfortable with it.

Many of us carry out hurts, anger, frustrations, depressions, limitations, ugly past, unforgiveness, and lots more on our head like the mentioned rich passenger on that flight.

If we don't sincerely let go of this unnecessary baggage, we end up sharing the future with them. We can bury our wounds so deep and for so long. Sooner or later, events or crises can trigger them and bring them to the forefront of our consciousness.

What do we do when they resurrect? We must rebury

them and let me rest, so we have to move on with our lives. Whatever people say or do, take a minute to pray and think, then respond. Exercise your power of choice. When the devil moves people to hate, you love. Break that cycle. They might respond that we do not understand what happened to you.

It is never what has happened to us that represents us; it is what we eventually do with ourselves that do. So, do not let others' actions determine the character you play in your own life story. Many of us battle from our past.

However, we find it difficult to dislodge them because of their source. Don't be afraid to call that source a liar if it conflicts with what God says about you. Otherwise, it will always feel like it has a right to occupy.

People who hurt you are powerless creatures who feed on their fears about you. Why will they hurt you in the first place if they do not envy you? You must not give them the power to leave you with excess baggage you do not need.

The greatest thing you can do that will defeat them is to tell them you have forgiven them. When you forgive people, who have wronged you genuinely, you have won. Success has no place in unforgiveness. Holding onto things can rob you of a beautiful life. Why subject yourself to suffering when you can release yourself from carrying unnecessary life baggage?

God asks us not to judge others and not to condemn them.

He asks us to remember that we are not perfect and should see each other with compassion and kindness. He asks us to forgive so that others forgive us as well.

To start your life afresh begins from the heart. When you stop thinking of what others think of you and start living your life, you have won. Come to think of it, what do men say you are? They have no right to place a ticket on your life because they feel privileged.

You are not the poor getting poorer, or the limited person, who cannot achieve something meaningful. That is not who you are on earth. You are the rich discovering his or their purpose on earth. What is in that bank account does not define your true identity.

We have seen people who rose from the slum to become the shakers and movers of this world through their influence and money. The picture you create of yourself is what life prints out for you. If you have the wrong picture before reading this book, take another mental picture of yourself?

The world will not stop for you if you refuse to move.

However, it drags you along and forces you to become who you are not. Take for instance, a beauty queen who allowed herself to become a drug addict. Within a short time, the beauty starts fading, and we only see the rot her lifestyle has subjected her to become.

Any day, she rediscovers herself and let go of her drug habit, her beauty will gradually return to her. That is how life treats us. When we forget who we are and start living contrary to whom we should become, things fall apart for us.

Do not allow the circumstances of life to decide how we must live on earth. Recreate a world that is full of beautiful dreams and start living in these dreams.

The life cycle is similar to the water cycle. What you give is what you receive.

CHAPTER 3

The Mirage

Have you woken up with a feeling of heaviness and felt that you would not survive the underlying cause of that situation? This type of helplessness often happens to us, but we still move past it. No matter the bruises such a situation leaves us with, it does not stop us from facing our present and future. This means no matter what you are passing through today, the future holds better days for you.

Just like a mirage, we speed past on a major road during a sunny day, so are our problems. For drivers who are not familiar with mirage's science, they tend to reduce their speed when they see mirages on the road. When we slow down for challenges to overwhelm us, we give in to depression and anxiety.

These two things do us no good; rather, they compound our problems for us. Matthew 6:30-33(MSG) says: *If God gives such attention to the appearance of wildflowers—*

most of which are never even seen—don't you think he'll attend to you, take pride in you, do his best for you? What I'm trying to do here is to get you to relax, not to be so preoccupied with getting, so you can respond to God's giving. People who don't know God and how he works fuss over these things, but you know both God and how he works. Steep your life in God-reality, God-initiative, God-provisions. Don't worry about missing out. You'll find all your everyday human concerns will be met.

How can you have this assurance and still panic when you have bills to pay. As scary as late payment can be, something is more assuring; the promises of God. Often, we forget we are in this world. We did not come to the scene to live miserable lives. You have a miraculous life that is unexplainable. When those around you complain about the economy, you tell yourself, 'My resources are from above. I live in the abundance of God's blessing.' One day, your positive affirmations will manifest and crown you with rewards of good works.

No matter how difficult things might be for you, you will come out victorious. A man called Jacob was a fraudster; he lived to reap from the hard work of others, including his brother. He did not spare his age-ridden father by collecting every blessing the man had saved all his life for his elder son. Yet, Jacob did not care about the feeling of those he defrauded until he met God.

He gave up his ugly past and refused to allow them to stop him from becoming a better person. Jacob buried his past mistakes and rough lifestyle; he refused to let self-condemnation ruin his life.

What past has stopped you from moving forward? Have you allowed guilt to crush you? When God spoke to Jacob, He did not remind him of his past. In God's eyes, the past was erased when Jacob gave them up for a higher life. I love how the Message Bible rendered his new relationship with God… *But you, Israel, are my servant. You're Jacob, my first choice, descendants of my good friend Abraham. I pulled you in from all over the world, called you in from every dark corner of the earth, telling you, 'You're my servant, serving on my side. I've picked you. I haven't dropped you. 'Don't panic. I'm with you. There's no need to fear, for I'm your God. I'll give you strength. I'll help you. I'll hold you steady, keep a firm grip on you.*

It does not matter how many times you failed in a project. If you have come to that point in life when you feel that God has abandoned you, take a step back, and reconsider His unfailing love. The resurrection life you received from God is not a timid, grave tending life.

It is adventurously expectant, greeting God with a childlike "What's next, Papa?" God's Spirit touches our spirits and confirms who we are. We know who he is, and we know who we are: Father and children. Also, we know we are going to get what is coming to us—an unbelievable inheritance! We go through exactly what Christ goes through. If we go through the hard times with him, then we are certainly going to go through the good times with him!

CHAPTER 4

The Sloth Race

Imagine your life moving in slow motion. While others speed through their careers, education, and life pursuits, you feel that everyone has left you. If we ever find ourselves in this unpleasant situation, we often compare other people's progress with ours. In the shortest time, depression sets in, and we tend to forget that we have different addresses in life.
The things we have achieved successfully suddenly becomes nothing. In the race of life, everyone has a lane. You can only drive yourself at your pace when you try to race against people who do not recognize that you are competing with them; the effort and time become wasteful.

Do not allow other people's testimonies to intimidate you. When you put yourself on the pedestal of others, you find yourself as a sloth racer. In this race, you race alone because no one is ready to join you.

Sloths are known for their preference of being heroic role models for laziness. While sloths are dubbed the animal kingdom's laziest, they live a remarkable life free of competing against others.

These remarkable animals have survived for millions of years despite being surrounded by predators, desperately seeking ways to take them off the earth. The life of a sloth is nothing a lazy human wish for an enemy.

Yet, they offer us life lessons that can change our lives forever. The life of the party and boisterous can be appealing. There are no dull moments, and people tend to gravitate toward them because of the exciting and experimental lifestyle.

However, sometimes, we find the most successful live the 'sloth life,' taking things easy, learning to reduce stress and worries, and knowing when to keep the rumbling talkative in their heads quiet.

The slot knows how to keep pushing for survival without focusing on the pain of rejection and limited movements. They do not allow those failures to lose out in projects or getting rejected closer to their success of getting to their destinations.

You do not have to act like a sloth to win your race. You have everything about life and godliness that will propel you to your countless victories. No destiny is accomplished without you making sacrifices. You cannot make a sacrifice without making tough decisions. You make tough decisions based on your convictions.

The conviction that keeps you going is not about what you want to achieve but why you want to achieve the result. Stop looking at your problems. The more you concentrate on your problems, the more you expand them to become a mountain. Think of how to step out of your situation. Change your focus and begin to rejoice to know that your breakthrough is on the way.

Most of us put money first as the means of our problems' ends. In truth, some situations require money to solve and no money to solve them. The first step of madness is repeatedly doing the same thing even when you know it is not working.

That is what happens when you overthink your challenges. Stop running yourself down each time you fail. There is a lot of value in your failure. Use those lessons learned to push yourself and do better next time.

When men say there is a casting down, things will not work out, refuse to accept the popular views, especially when it affects you. Tell yourself you are coming out of such a situation without bruises.

CHAPTER 5

Lessons from sloths

I Know Who I am

Do you know why you are where you are today? Can you tell yourself who you are? When people tell you 'I know who I am,' they are simply affirming that they know themselves regardless of the situation they find themselves in. You made a mistake, and it seems it has soiled your life. Does that mean you cannot erase these mistakes by starting all over?
No one has the power to bring you down with hurting words. When you hear people tell you that 'you are not qualified, undeserving, a no-body, and other degrading words,' never take it to heart.

You had put in a lot of work in a project, worked selflessly, and sacrificed so much, and you got 'fired or sacked.' As painful as that situation might be, do not be dismayed. Do not compromise your standard because you got ill-maltreated.

The best person you can always become is to maintain your belief in doing good works for others.

Things might not seem favorable for a while, but your reward will surely come. When it does, you will forget the pain and devastation that happened during your crisis.

Embrace the Role of a Creator

When you were born on earth, you came helpless and needy. You depended on others until you were emancipated from the phase of dependence. Today, you have conquered many wars and were rewarded by life with more wars, in the form of the challenges you are facing today.

When life creates a difficult terrain for you, recreate the situation with a positive attitude and a winning spirit. You are the creator of what you want in life. When you find yourself in a 'sloth' situation and things seem to stagnate, reassure yourself that the situation is for a short period.

Do not give up! Keep patience as a friend and work to become better than your yesterday. Do not be scared to get back up. Learn to dream again, to love again, and to try again.

Life's best lessons often come at our worst mistakes and worst moments.

When everything seems to go wrong, and you feel like

you are in a rut forever, remind yourself that you are bigger than that situation. If you feel like quitting, remember the sloths' way of doing things. They keep focus and move towards their goals irrespective of their limitations. We often assume that the worst will sleep us away, but we still come around to better days.

Find the strength to live better every day. Find the courage to laugh when life hits hard on you.

Therefore, I tell you, do not be anxious about your life, what you will eat or what you will drink, nor about your body, what you will put on. Is not life more than food and the body more than clothing? And which of you, by being anxious, can add a single hour to his span of life?

Make peace with imperfection.

Sloths accept their imperfection yet work towards perfection by taking advantage of every opportunity they find in their environment to survive—things you cannot do, let them be and move on with your life.

You should attempt to do something and fail than do nothing at all. It is not over because you lost; it is over when you complain and do nothing about your situation. If you believe in something, go for it. Do not allow the past to stop you from taking up opportunities. Sometimes, life shut doors in your face because it is time for you to move forward. Many of us would not take a step into the unknown unless circumstances present themselves to us.

The challenges around you may seem unbearable. The world may look as if it is about to collapse on you. You may be losing grip on that hope that should have pushed you forward. Take a deep breath and tell yourself, 'everything will be alright.' Do we mean you should stop worrying over the impending issues? Of course, no one worries and wins an award.

How many times have you failed in a project? Maybe, you have come to a point in life when it seems like God has abandoned you. You have the inherent ability to succeed no matter the challenges facing you. You can do anything you put your mind to. We see many crumbled marriages, careers, and dreams every day because we have failed to see the ray of hope in the future.

Today is just a day among the millions of days in our world. If today is not bright, tomorrow would be bright. It all boils down to having hope and faith in what you do. There is only one life for us; why spend it in worries and lack? The route of success has nothing to do with lack. When you have a lack mentality, you have a weak future.

**Commit your work to the Lord, and
your plans will be established.**

CHAPTER 6

When we hear the word ' impossible, most of us resign our fate without making an effort to discredit it. When do things become impossible? For you, when you resign your fate that you have lost because a situation has become impossible? We have advanced technology because some people are working on things many of us believe is impossible. Does impossible exist?

We are timeless men controlling time.

Take, for instance, how do prophecies come to reality for those that believe in them? Prophecy or prediction of the future has always happened. Whether we believe in it or not, we have seen predictions happen when experts in any field say things in future tense. What about prophecies about your life?

When people tell you that you have a great future, you are smart, overcomer, and so on, what do you do after hearing such words? Do you take them as mere words that someone who doesn't understand your situation is saying?

What you do with prophecies matters most. Some scientists have broken ancient landmarks records because they refused to follow the norm.

Refuse to allow people's conclusion of a matter to get to you. That a group of people fails in a business does not mean that you will fail if you take a different approach.

Prophecies are like plants that must be watered. For it to come to fulfillment, you have to nurture it to believe in it. The moment your dreams or prophecies are out of your way, it will slip your hands. Prophecies are fragile to handle. You must handle it with care, prayers, and hope that it must grow fast for you to reap its fruits.

Speak positive words to yourself. Believe that all things are possible for you. It does not matter how things might look when you say great words concerning you, your kids, partner, job, environment, and life; continue saying it until everything responds to you. Like a magnet, words get attracted to things you push them to.

What have people said about you that have refused to accommodate good news to you? Sink every contrary word or situation that refuses to conform to what you desire. Erase those impossible thoughts and write possibilities in every situation surrounding you.

Certain things that happen to us does not mean we are

imperfect. It does not mean we did something wrong. Sometimes, we have done the right things and hoped for the best, when we find our walls start crumbling. All these things that are pressing on you are only telling you to warm up for your testimonies.

Do not allow yourself to be intimidated by the testimonies of others. That your friends have gotten amazing news does not mean yours will not come. God who created you knows your beginning to the end. Do not divert from your course; keep on with your movement.

You do not detect to God how he will solve your problem. God is your competitive advantage. When God changes your state, your estate changes. Promotion starts coming. People who know you will wonder what has happened to you. You are a solution going somewhere to happen.

"Once you choose hope, anything is possible." Anonymous

Probably the most striking hindrance to why many of us do not succeed in some aspects of our life is because of a lack of self-belief. We have believed more in negativity and bad news that we find it difficult to embrace what seems more challenging for our minds to handle.

Whatever our minds can believe, we can achieve. If you must believe the impossible, you just have to work on what you believe.

The mind is so powerful that it can deliver anything we set our desire upon. The mind can only make the impossible to be possible if we believe only in possibilities. You should have positive expectations and practice positive talking sessions.

Learn to have your mind rewired to positive expectations. When you train your unconscious mind to defeat fear, challenges, depression, anger, and negative vibes, it becomes more powerful than you can imagine.

Have a stubborn faith that does not see stumbling blocks on your way. When it comes to stumbling situations, it walks through it, believing only the best to happen. When your mind operates on this frequency, dreams come to reality, challenges gradually fizzle away, and you will have reasons to be grateful for life.

Nothing is impossible for the person with strong conviction and ready to act on that conviction. If you have a conviction and refuse to work on it, you might not find it easy to actualize that project. Successful people act immediately, and they have a conviction to do something.

Act as if you have achieved. When you condition your mind to believe you have conquered your challenges, it frees you from the unnecessary baggage hanging over you. For you to win in life, you must act and speak success.

The mistake we often make is that we allow life challenges to dominate us. The problems of this life do not have an end. The more we conquer challenges, the bigger challenges we face. While punishing yourself over what you are going through? Tomorrow has another assignment for you. You do not want to lag when others are flying with their success stories.

You must believe that impossibilities are possible for you. The power of your belief is within your control to regulate. You decide what you want your mind to believe.

CHAPTER 7

Keep Winning

**What shall we then say to these things? If
God be for us, who can be against us?**

Do you ever feel like things are stacked against you? Have you considered the people that succeeded despite the odds? If these people can come out victorious at the end of their dark tunnels, who said you could not overcome your adversities? In life, learn not to be afraid of your situation, critics, or adversaries because they do not matter in your quest for winning.

Irrespective of what is happening around you, trying to drown your voice, frustrate you, and make you shed tears, do not stop growing. Do not stop moving. The more these distractions become powerful, the less glorious your life will become. Give these contrary factors less to feed on your fear and vulnerability.

No situation bothers a failure who has nothing to lose failing again

When you are faced with challenges that seem impossible, stand boldly in front of your mind and tell yourself, 'I am a success!'

Detractors or adversaries found your address because you are a stumbling block to them. They see you as a threat. In an attempt to derail you and get at you, have no fear because you are making progress in your race.

Remain focus and keep doing what you are doing, while they keep stumbling as you make progress. You can do all things you put your mind to achieve through Christ, who gives you the strength.

If your mind has not been trained to embrace the winning mentality, it might be difficult to allow yourself to accept some uplifting words. Take, for instance, a child who grew up in a home where positive words and the mentality of a winner are thrown at, becomes daring and ready to take on the world.

If you let the child know that he/she cannot fail, even when that child has a shortcoming, you encourage that child to move on without looking behind. What do you think will become of that child?

Cultivate the habit of a winner's mentality, irrespective of the situation. Whatever you have set your mind to do, you can do it. Come to terms with the truth that you can overcome everything standing like a giant in front of you.

"Now unto him, that can do exceedingly abundantly above all that we ask or think, according to the power that worketh in us, unto him be glory in the church by Christ Jesus throughout all ages, world without end. Amen"

You should practice this confession. It does not matter that you made a mistake while trying to win. Do not be discouraged because you are learning to become a life champion; soon enough, you will perfect the act of winning.

What about the wasted years? How do you make things right again? Do you believe in a miracle? God can restore your lean years; He can restore your wasted moments and make you new. There is a certain mentality you should have to win in life; it is the mentality of winning, where you know that come what may, victory is assured. Be strong and courageous as you step out every morning.

Someone might say, 'How can I think this way when I have nagging problems trying to bring me to my knees?' 'But we get discouraged or depressed sometimes?' How can you be discouraged or depressed when you are one with the Lord? You are a god! Be rest assured that life will throw tantrums at you. How do you handle a child throwing tantrums in public? Give no room for situations to take away your joy. Nothing should be able to stop your joy because you are shinning every day.

Never find yourself depressed or discouraged. Learn to put up a smiling face amid the raging storms of life. Do not criticize yourself for what people have done or said against you. The Lord is your light and salvation; whom shall you fear?

Refuse to accept anything short of a life of success and victory. The world may be facing hardship, but you are living in a different atmosphere. You dwell in an atmospheric covering of safety, peace, and victory.

Say this:

I am eternally victorious. I have power over crises; I am manifesting dominion and prospering exceedingly. I live far above the distracting elements of this world because I live in a place called Christ.

CHAPTER 8

Keeping Faith in Hard Times

Through much in 64 years of living on earth, Patricia had been a British-Ghanaian immigrant who has never visited Ghana since she was born. As a child, she barely survived, having been born prematurely. The doctors told her mum to give up on her because she suffered from Potter's Syndrome. The mum had a stubborn faith that the doctors cannot tell her to terminate a baby she had after 23 years of childlessness.

She left the doctor's office and never came back. Patricia was born in preterm. She survived every childhood sickness that could have taken her life. She was deeply religious, but the good things of life seemed not to come to her path.

The more she tried to escape hardship, the more challenging life became. She got married at 52 to the love of her life and had their baby, Jameson, at 62. Things were beginning to look beautiful for her and her husband when Covid-19 struck. They were in Paris for her first vacation in life when she started feeling unwell. They came to London, and the family came down with the virus. She lost her husband and son in a two days interval. Life ended for her. People come to console her often, but the faith they try to rebuild for her is so fragile and breaks before they can leave her house. What do we tell Patricia? How do we console her and tell her that God loves her more?

For I know the plans I have for you, declares the Lord, plans for welfare and not for evil, to give you a future and a hope. Jeremiah 29:11

Friends, we know that life can be sunshine and roses, and sometimes, it can be dark. No matter how we try to behave as if nothing has happened, we still feel the pain. Whether you are struggling with your faith or asking if God cares for you, it is something we can talk about.

When trials and difficult times envelop us, we find ourselves fighting temptation and often begin to sink as our faith gives in to despair and fear. Every moment of joy and victory we have achieved over the years suddenly gets drowned in the fearful voices screaming in our heads.

We try to escape these problems during the day, doing so many things to numb the challenges and get stuck in the night, feeling like we are carrying the world's burdens.

When morning comes, we feel beaten and caged with misery. The circle repeats over and over until we lose faith in what we once believed.

To rule your world and stand above every situation, you must continuously remain active in your relationship with God. Your faith must stay strong, no matter what you face. Make it a habit to keep your faith and move with hope rather than despair.

Outside God is an endless tunnel that is too dark that one can only see the light if God shows up. However, God does not show up at your doorsteps if you do not invite him over. God plans to have a father and child relationship with you.

Imagine allowing God to handle everything concerning you. The time to quit doubting is now. Take a step back and come home to your God. Life is safer in God than when you live in doubt. When we look at what is happening around the world, it can be scary. Some of the things we witness seem so unreal; some look like scripts playing out in a weird movie or fiction novel.

These strange occurrences, terrorism, insecurity, economic and health crisis, leave one wondering what next plague is coming. Many people wake with a suspicion of the worst. Was this the world created for us? Why is God allowing all these terrible things to happen?

Come unto me all ye that labour and are heavy laden, and I will give you rest, God is saying to you now.

There is much hope ahead. The future is beautiful for those who take shelter under God's wings. We have victory in God. We talk to you because Jesus Christ is the good shepherd; he cannot leave us as orphans for calamities to crash us. He is close behind us in our struggle; He does not look away when we fall and start all over again.

The scriptures are replete with mind-blowing information that shows us how God has offered us a victorious life ahead. We have nothing to fear. Refuse to accept anything contrary to a life of glory and success in Christ Jesus.

The death of Jesus Christ wasn't for nothing; He died to give you life. He became poor that you may become rich in Christ; he was bruised for you to have health and by His stripes, you have become healed. You are the righteousness of Christ Jesus. Therefore, you have an excellent mind, an extraordinary life, and divine life.

The world may be facing an unpredictable time, but you live a higher life that supersedes this world's governance. Trust God to take care of your situation. Trust him to help you pay off your loans or mortgage.

Even if you are in great debt, trust him to pay off the debt. Give up your struggles, pain, challenges, sickness, and negativity, and hand it over to Jesus Christ. There is one thing He requires of you, which is to seek ye first the kingdom of God, and his righteousness and all these things shall be added unto you.

For you to live by faith is a free-will choice. You have

to choose God's way over your own and trust Him to help you. It is about holding firm your faith in every situation. Are you presently fighting to hold onto your faith? Are you in a situation where positive words have refused to make meaning? Does it seem as if God has left you behind?

The testing of faith can be the most difficult situation to handle as a human. Whom do you run to when everything seems to have failed? No situation is too big for God to handle. You may think that God is not acting fast or has not shown up the way you wanted him to.

Stop questioning everything you once believed and start believing that God cannot bring shame to you.

Refuse to allow anything to distract your attention away from the Lord. Set your attention and affection on Him. Trust Him with your situation and life, including your doubts, and allow him to synchronize your life with His perfect will.

CHAPTER 9

Some people have struggled all their lives to make things work out for them. Some have to pray for everything to happen. What others get without work; they have to work extra hard to get it. Many people have lived in want and lack for so long and find it difficult to believe in better days.

The problem is with their minds because they have accepted that everything must be done with prayers and hard work. You can live beyond your limits. There is no crime for thinking beyond your status. Life can box you into a hole; it is your responsibility to climb out of that hole.

Think and talk about success. God did not create you to heap suffering and struggling on your head. He did not plan for you a miserable life.

For you know the grace of our Lord Jesus Christ, that, though He was rich, yet for your sakes, He becomes poor, that ye through His poverty might be rich.

The world is not getting stable; the more the government is trying to quench plague or handle their economic plights, the more they find more problems to solve. Why must you be at the center of each crisis? You have a life that has been ordained for greatness and success.

When trouble comes, you have the inherent ability to make tremendous changes that work in your favour.

But you are a chosen race, a royal priesthood, a dedicated nation, [God's] own purchased, special people, that you may set forth the wonderful deeds and display the virtues and perfections of Him who called you out of darkness into His marvelous light. 1 Peter 2:9

Reread the above verse. The tense used in the phrase is a present happening and not a futuristic promise. Can you see why your life must be excellent? God carefully chose you like royalty. Forget everything happening around you. Resist the temptation that is telling otherwise about the impending problems.

How do you process the above promise from God? Believing is a choice. You have been perfected to display God's wonderful deeds around you. Yes, there is no denying that things are not that rosy. However, He is faithful that promises you the good things of life. You have been blessed to be a blessing to your world.

God's desire is for you to be a winner no matter the circumstances. Have you witnessed a last-minute miracle? Things were going haywire to destruction, and that timely text message or phone call changed your life.

The doctors have told you that they have given up on a permanent solution to your health-related issues and placed you on a life drug routine. The judgment of that doctor becomes your death sentence. What do you think of God's power to heal you? Does that mean you were created to suffer throughout life?

What are you saying to yourself? And God can make all grace abound toward you; that ye, always having all sufficiency in all things, may abound to every good work.

Enough of the suffering! Start seeing yourself in a different situation and start rejecting every contrary situation to a life of excellence.

There are people in distress and pain whose healing can be perfected if they look away from their pains and needs and pray for others. It does not matter what has happened to you or where you have been; allow God to take over. Yield to the dominion of the supernatural by practicing faith proclamation and meditation.

What can you see? You can start practicing seeing visions of your new life, a life free of pain, lack, difficulty, and disappointments. If you have visions of sickness, fear, failure, and poverty, reject them and switch your mind to visions of what you want. When you practice this, you will be amazed at how your life can change for the positive.

You have the responsibility to make yourself happier. When you give in to depression, anxiety, and sadness, things aggravate those moods and leave you worse than you started. When the squeeze is on, and everything seems to work against you, laugh, Laugh aloud and tell the situation that you are more than a conqueror.

How does it look at someone who lost his house, failed his examinations, got divorced, and was unable to pay bills is joyous?

Most people will believe the person has lost his mind to misfortunes, while those will believe he is in shock. The more they try to make him realize his deplorable condition, the more he tells them that 'things are well with him.'

How we manage our situation depends on what we want to achieve. The man who lost everything to misfortune might be seeing a future that none of us saw in him. Is it possible to have a future without worries? With student loans leaving us helpless, mortgages that have left us on a tight budget, or life demands that have refused to stop coming hard at us, what do we do with the future?

How can a future be without worries when we have unresolved situations following us to the future? Life in Christ Jesus is bigger than a future that is tainted by the unpalatable experience. No situation is too difficult for God to clean up and make worth enjoying. Everything is on our heads.

"For I know the plans I have for you," declares the Lord,

"plans to prosper you and not to harm you, plans to give you hope and a future." Clean your head of negativity and fill it up with beautiful thoughts...Being confident of this, that he who began a good work in you will carry it on to completion until the day of Christ.

Finally, trust in the Lord with all your heart and lean not on your understanding; in all your ways submit to him, and he will make your life beautiful. For those light and momentary troubles squeezing, you achieve a great future with no business with your challenges.

Never be afraid to trust an unknown future to a know God. -Corrie ten Boom

CHAPTER 10

You are called to live a life of no worries about what the future holds. The wind might be turbulent, but your flight would land safely. Since worries have not fetched you money or made your situation better, why not try trusting in the Lord?

God brings death, and God brings life, brings down to the grave, and raises up. God brings poverty, and God brings wealth; he lowers, he also lifts up. He puts poor people on their feet again; he rekindles burned-out lives with fresh hope, Restoring dignity and respect to their lives— a place in the sun! For the very structures of earth are God's; he has laid out his operations on a firm foundation. He protectively cares for his faithful friends, step by step, but leaves the wicked to stumble in the dark. No one makes it in this life by sheer muscle! God's enemies will be blasted out of the sky, crashed in a heap, and burned. God will set things right all over the earth; he'll give strength to his king, he'll set his anointed on top of the world!

You are a royal priesthood and specially chosen by God. If God be for you, who can stand in your way of success? Philippians 4:6-7(MSG) made it easier for you to tell you what to do when you feel like worrying. Do not fret or worry. Instead of worrying, pray. Let petitions and praises shape your worries into prayers, letting God know your concerns. Before you know it, a sense of God's wholeness, everything coming together for good, will come and settle you down. It is wonderful what happens when Christ displaces worry at the center of your life.

Count your blessings and name them one after the other. Amid every fierce storm, God has marked you out to survive.

Do not let the devil take your shine away. You are special. You should stop feelings from detecting your life for you. What people say about you makes no difference. What matters most is what you have said about yourself, life, family, and business. For you are God's workmanship, created in Christ Jesus unto good works, which God has before ordained that you should walk in them.

In a few words, tell God you have come to say thank you for everything He has done for you. If you are hurting, healing has come to you. For those who are sick in their bodies, take a bold step by talking your way out of that ailment. The choice to live a higher life has been offered by God, take it and run with it. You are a blessing to bless others. Do not allow circumstances to deter you from living your life to its fullness.

Finally, my brethren, whatsoever things are true, whatsoever things are honest, whatsoever things are just, whatsoever things are pure, whatsoever things are lovely, whatsoever things are of good report; if there be any virtue, and if there be any praise, think on these things.

ABOUT THE AUTHOR

Gideon Okeoma

Gideon is a teacher of the word of God. He believes that all humans are created in the image of God and have divine ability.

He encourages people to renew their mind through God's word to enable them to know the will and plan of God for their lives.

Gideon's mission is to impact generations with the simplicity of the Gospel of our Lord Jesus Christ.

He is married to his loving wife Lilian and they are blessed with three beautiful daughters, Glory, Grace, Gift,

Gideon can be reached through pastorgideon@hotmail.com

Another book from Gideon
Sacred Lover Vol.1